THE EIGHTEEN YEARS
THAT DIDN'T
CHANGE ANYTHING

a memoir.

ENRICO TESLA

Copyright © 2022 Enrico Tesla

All rights reserved.

No part of this book may be reproduced or used in any manner without written permission of the copyright owner except for the use of quotations in a book review.

Cover and interior layout by Blue Pen

ISBN: 978-1-7397084-0-5 (hardcover)
ISBN: 978-1-7397084-1-2 (paperback)
ISBN: 978-1-7397084-2-9 (ebook)

Published by Young Prometheus Publications

ABSTRACT

I was distracted. My gaze stumbled upon the ugly. I chose not to look away.

CONTENTS

Introduction 1
  What is death? 1
  Procreation. 2
  The fight 3
  One fight. Many fights 3
  The birth of culture 4
  New environments. New skills 5
  The winning skills within an advanced society 6

Summer 1999 9
  Bologna 9
  Friendship 10
  Mediation and dissimulation 12
  Courtly love 12
  The conglomerate of networks 13
  The champion of the weak ones 14
  Relax the competition 15
  My father 16
  Summer 1999: my status 17
  Summer 1999: the job and the crew 18
  Summer 1999: the girls 18
  Summer 1999: trouble in sight 19
  Summer 1999: the win 20
  Summer 1999: the loss 21
  Summer 1999: the isolation 22

Summer 1999: trauma 23
Summer 1999: my analysis 23
Summer 1999: genes............................ 24
Summer 1999: suicide 25
Summer 1999: is there a way out? 26
My life's cycle................................. 26
Maximize my potential 27
Changing the environment I was in.............. 29

Summer 2017 31
The absolute................................... 31
The introduction of relativism................... 32
What is success? 32
Time: the healer................................ 34
The conclusion of my experience in Italy.......... 35
Why England................................... 35
Welcome to London 37
My life in the United Kingdom.................. 38
My career 39
Ms. S. 40
The date....................................... 41
Humor and human intelligence 43
Our relationship progresses..................... 44
Economic wellness and stability 44
Why isn't the telephone ringing?................. 45
My manager's birthday party.................... 46
Heart racing................................... 47
No action 49
New status 50

Our first argument	51
The bliss	52
Ms. S.'s aspirations	53
The discrepancy	54
The inner conflict	54
Ms. S. leaves me	55
Who was Ms. S.? - part one	56
Who was Ms. S.? - part two	57
Why I loved Ms. S.	59
The break-up: its effects on me	60
What is trauma?	60
"Get busy living"	61
My decision	62
Being strong socially	63
Is she with my manager?	64
Dissection of a humiliation	65
A social convention: don't engage romantically with your friend's ex-girlfriend	66
The likelihood they were together	67
Would he tell me?	68
I suspect she's with my manager	69
"Are you with my ex-girlfriend?"	70
Who was my manager?	72
Our professional disagreement	73
Additional signs they could be together	75
Observing my manager's behavior	76
A park close to her home	77
Her birthday	78

- Would it matter if I knew? 79
- The winner 80
- Conclusion 83
  - The theory of evolution is science. 83
  - The law of natural selection is the rightful lens to interpret our lives as well as all human history .. 84
  - Culture is a tool 85
  - Morality and law: the concepts of good and evil ... 87
  - Morality and law: regularity and evolution 87
  - Beyond good and evil. 89
  - The Absolute 90
  - Einstein's equation 90
  - Space and movement 91
  - The discrepancy 92
  - Inert matter and life 92
  - Physical laws and biological laws 93
  - A consideration over the question of the meaning of life 94
  - Criminality, addiction, loneliness, mental illness, and suicide 95
  - Psychologists 96
  - Non-hetero sexualities 98
  - Me after Ms. S. 100
  - This book 102
  - Now. 103

INTRODUCTION

What is death?

I was already dead when I started to write. I wonder. When is a man dead? Do we die? Of course, we do. Human beings die each day. We die as a personality. A bundle of experiences and point of views. We don't die biologically. At least, if we reproduce ourselves.

I wonder. Human beings with all their memories and feelings die. Or, at least, so it appears. Dying means termination. No more. No matter how much we fought during our lives. All seems lost. Several times, discussing with my peers, I contended human life equals learning. That is: The only common denominator I find in our existences is this constant process of accumulation and elaboration of experiences. We don't change. We evolve. We cannot get rid of our baggage. All is lost with our death, though. Or, at least, so it appears.

What is the meaning of life, then? What has got

significance within it? Significance is what is enduring time. Significance cannot be what is passing.

Life is like a petrol engine with its phases: birth; eat, sex, sleep; eat, sex, sleep; eat, sex, sleep; death. The machine is perfect. It always comes back to its original phase. Until it breaks down. Nothing is left.

Except.

We may procreate. Yes, procreate. This is the only achievement that will allow for a part of us to carry forward. The only segment that can overcome our termination point.

There is no other scientific reason to life than to reproduce ourselves. Any other objective we may wish to assign to it is merely an opinion.

Procreation

There is a law in nature. We discovered it some time ago. This law tells us that just the fittest will procreate. Not the fittest in absolute terms (can we even define this concept?) but the most capable with regard to their own environments.

As well the expression "the fittest will procreate" does not refer to one generation. It is a long-term process. A lot of fools reproduce each day. Yet, over an extended period of time, just the genes of the best will be passed on.

The fittest are the ones that most likely will

reproduce. They are the ones that can protect themselves and their descendants the most. The lineage of the accidental procreators can be interrupted at each generation.

The fight

Life is a fight. A struggle to overcome all our opponents and to reproduce ourselves.

This conflict is not outside us. It is us. It permeates every action and every instinct of each living being.

The law of natural selection is a physical law. It is as compelling and pervasive as gravity. As we cannot correctly interpret a movement without taking into consideration the latter, it's also true we are not able to intimately understand life without factoring in the former.

One fight. Many fights

We are engaged in a deadly fight within our species for self-preservation and reproduction. At the same time, as a species, we are locked in a similar struggle with other kinds.

We tend to forget about this second contest today, such is the advantage and control we appear to have on other species. Nevertheless, this fight is still real, as we draw our livelihood from the same natural resources.

The struggle between species and the one between individuals are strictly interlocked to each other. That is: The former defines the plateau on which the latter is fought on. If a species prevails on the others, then a wider proportion of its members will flourish via natural selection. Conversely, if we are part of a losing kind, our chances to survive will diminish.

The birth of culture

Sometimes I imagine how it must have been at the dawn of man. What were the chances of humankind surviving? Every species has its strong point. Some have physical strength; some are fast; some can camouflage; some can inject you with a deadly venom.

What was mankind's strong point? Human beings have got large brains. This means we don't just perceive our environment; we also store it in our mind. As long as I can hold a picture of my surroundings, I can operate on it. I can turn it and twist it at my advantage. Mankind is the toolmaker: from the sharpened rock to the spaceship. Through the use of tools, a human being is stronger, faster, and deadlier of the strongest, fastest, and deadliest of all the animals.

There are material tools; there are, also, immaterial instruments. Science, politics, and economic theory are examples of the latter ones. Equally to physical devices, their purpose is to increase mankind's effectiveness on nature. They achieve this objective by different means: such as minimizing social conflict or eviscerating the laws that underpin the development of the physical world and society.

We call culture any elaboration of nature produced by mankind, either material or immaterial: from the wooden spear to the string theory.

Culture is not ontologically different from nature. It is just one of its proceedings. Human culture is not substantially dissimilar from a termites' mound or a beaver's dam. They are all transformations of nature created by animals with the objective to survive. They just feel different because of the quantity and degree of the elaboration achieved by humans.

New environments. New skills

Culture, nature's daughter, has interacted with its mother since its birth. The pair has dialectically evolved over time.

Humanity lives in an ever-changing mixture of nature and culture. This has been true since the birth of civilization. This blend varies by time and location so that, by now, we can say humanity has experienced and overcome an infinite number of settings.

The law of natural selection states just the fittest within a specific environment will survive. This implies mankind has dialectically evolved with the surroundings it has lived into. Within each condition, a certain number of champions have been celebrated.

We have to assume, barring any adaptability, individuals that have been successful within a certain environment would have not achieved the same results in another setting. Intuitively, this statement is more likely to be true wider is the difference between the environments considered.

The winning skills within an advanced society

What skills do you need to win in an advanced society? I bet a lot of you reading this book would love to know the answer to this question.

It is easy to think that at the start of the human history, when the natural element was making up the totality of our environment, our physical abilities would have been dominant in determining our chances to survive and reproduce ourselves. Later, when the background of our lives was made up more and more by other individuals of our species and by our artifacts, one might assume that the importance of this component, within the scope of natural selection, would have steadily declined.

So, what skills do you need to succeed today? Our society is extremely complex and stratified. It is formed by an infinite variety of institutions, products, and people. In order to win, our mind must possess the energy and capability to quickly acknowledge and understand whichever element it comes across. Equally, it must be able to promptly devise and deliver a course of action that effectively extracts what we need from our counterparts.

Our cognitive capability is critical for our success in our contemporary world. Nevertheless, many other components will participate in the determination of our personal outcome: from our physical appearance to our health, from our capacity to refine and maintain our faculties over time to sheer casualty.

In the end, we face the environment as an ever-changing bundle of energy and skills. It is the particular outcome of this interaction that will determine if we will or will not prevail.

SUMMER 1999

Bologna

A long time ago, I was a young man in Bologna. Beautiful city! I was coming from a town on the coast. I went there to study. It was the first time I left my parents' home, and I was in charge of my life.

What a gorgeous period! It is nice when you are young and full of energy. Your brain is constantly developing, and you feel you've reached a much more exhaustive understanding of the world you live in. You become filled with self-confidence. It was a time of discovery and growth. Splendid!

However, I had been struggling for a period of time. My relationships with others didn't come as spontaneously as I wanted. I felt like my mind was not engaged in my day-to-day life. Hence, I could hardly win an argument of any pedestrian nature.

Friendship

It occurred to me that I did not have many friends. I couldn't say there was that general consensus about my persona I would have desired. Many did not fear me. Hence, they didn't respect me. Others didn't find me interesting. Therefore, arguments and relationship breakdowns were a periodic recurrence in my life.

What is friendship? It is my opinion humanity only embrace science on the surface. Science itself is too complicated for the average woman or man. The way we know science is through slogans. We don't intimately understand it and its corollaries.

Science is knowledge that is both universal and necessary. That is: Firstly, it must be acknowledged by any rational being; secondly, it doesn't change over time.

Darwin's theory of evolution by means of natural selection is part of this knowledge. Yet, once the theory has been proven and accepted as part of the scientific truth, we still struggle to acknowledge all its implications.

Darwin's theory tells us the sole objective of life is to pass on our genetic pool through reproduction. It also teaches us that not all individuals will reach this objective. Just the ones that best adapt to their surroundings will do so.

This is a fact. As long as Darwin's is the current

science no other knowledge that contradict it or its corollaries can be accepted as truth or simply valid. Any alternative conception about the workings of life would have to displace the theory of evolution before to be considered.

What is friendship, therefore? It would be inconsistent with Darwin's theory if we were to tell each other it is the uninterested and altruistic love toward another human being. This is a love that has a return. Human beings build friendships, as they provide them with a better chance to survive and reproduce themselves. To be winners. A large net of friends means a large protection system. It means that someone who is antagonizing me is, in fact, alienating a vast group of people. Would you really do that? It is much easier to pick them individually. Isn't it?

More friends, more information. A friend will notify you when a good job, in the field you are looking for, is coming up. Sometimes this is all you need to transform and permanently improve your life. Sometimes a friend may even be key in you getting that job. Wouldn't it be nice?

In accordance with the law of natural selection, we thrive to be part of a net of friends. We are willing to spend our time and our resources to help a peer under the undeclared condition, we will get similar service in return when needed. We acknowledge we are stronger as part of a group.

Mediation and dissimulation

We can't talk of friendship in these terms in our day-to-day existence, though. The priority of the fight to survive and reproduce ourselves cannot be brought to life in front of us. The competition must be dissimulated. If we don't do it, human beings would be in a state of constant all-out war between each other. Nature has become culture. Yeast has become alcohol.

Humans learned this long ago. It is dictated by the same law of natural selection. Mediation limits conflict between individuals and it is the precondition for us to put together our strengths and our knowledge. It betters us as a species, and it allows us to prevail on all the other ones.

Culture is the unique elaboration of nature created by human beings. One of its key objectives is the need to restrain human conflict. Our concept of friendship and solidarity is one of the many tools it has generated to reach this finality.

Courtly love

I remember, many years ago, when I was in high school, being surprised to read the magnificent poetry of the High Middle Ages celebrating courtly love had originally been prompted by the pope seeking to hide the decadence of the clergy in the Provence region of France. The poems were praising love as the most ethereal and unselfish feeling. What was going on was a much more physical and hedonistic version of it. The sublime poetry was a smokescreen, a palliative for the public.

Yet, this does not deny that, after the inducted spark, the poets that followed were genuinely inspired by that concept of love. They completely ignored what started the literary genre they belonged to.

This is culture for human beings. We are born into it, and it is our second skin. We cannot even contemplate it as a possibility, a choice, an instrument that we have kept and developed just because of the results it delivers to us.

The conglomerate of networks

Back in Bologna, I believe, at some level, life had already showed me signs I had been selected. I had a network of friends, but I wasn't the most popular person around. You see: People want friends, but they look for "fit" companions. We need to be surrounded by successful people to bring ourselves up. "Weak" individuals may be more of a burden than an asset.

Society is a conglomeration of everchanging networks. Some of them are more extent and powerful; others are smaller and weaker. Some of them have a lot of interaction; some of them have few.

Every day we fight to earn the membership of the network we belong to. At the same time, we thrive to gain access to a more powerful and influential group. We join it if we are granted permission and we believe we can sustain the new affiliation in the long run. Conversely, we are pushed out from a network if we are not effective enough in our action. We are forced, then, to join a weaker group or, eventually, to be alone.

The champion of the weak ones

We experience that some people appear to purposely seek the company of the weak ones. They stand by them. Some of these individuals may even come from wealthy and powerful backgrounds. It seems like they are voluntarily proceeding from strength to vulnerability.

The fact that we aim to be part of a more powerful and influential group is in line with the law of natural selection. This affiliation, in fact, would increase the chances to survive and prosper of ourselves and our lineage. The idea that some individuals would intentionally proceed in the opposite direction would undermine the current science.

We need to dig deeper. We ought to understand the background of the champions of the weak ones. Do they feel secure in their initial social position? Do they think they can sustain their affiliation for a long period? Are they, indeed, alone and looking to join a network?

The champions of the weak ones' opportunity to be part of a powerful group is just claimed and self-declared. These individuals, in fact, do not have one. They don't have the option to withhold to a more powerful position. Their only choice is between a weak network and loneliness. They just pick the lesser of the two evils.

Relax the competition

The champions of the losers are no different from anyone else: They want to win. Yet, they realize they cannot achieve this result within the current setting. They need to change the way the battle is fought.

They create the morality of the weak ones. Within it, competition in society is condemned and vulnerability is celebrated. Their intent is to shuffle the social order and, through it, install themselves at the top. This, in turn, will allow for a part of natural resources been shifted from the current owners to them.

The morality of the weak ones is just another tool to fight in the social struggle. Just think at the animal realm. Look how many different techniques are deployed to prevail. If you are a chameleon, you cannot fight your predators by true force. You will need to come up with something different and, if necessary, even far-fetched to survive.

My father

Trying to undermine social competition is an old approach to fight other human beings. It is normally adopted by individuals who have been pushed at the margins of society and that, now, see in a relaxation of the public conflict a way to facilitate their clawing back to its center.

I remember, when I still was a child, my father declaring bankruptcy for his business. I know now this affected him very deeply. One afternoon around that period, I was a passenger in his car. We stopped on the side of a heavy traffic road. We were waiting for someone or something: I don't remember now. I do recall, though, that my father, instead of staying in the car, got out, put on a carnival mask on his face and stood in front of the cars that were passing by. Of course, many of the drivers laughed: some with him; some at him.

I believe that was his way to fight back. He didn't give up on life and happiness. He didn't want to become a social pariah. He wanted to point out how life is absurd—the same life he was contesting so intensely until few days before. He did it in the hope to get a break from society; an open door through which squeeze himself back into it.

Summer 1999: my status

I don't know exactly what changed in the summer of 1999, but, I remember, I started that season with a new purpose in my mind. I wanted to provide my life with a sharp upturn. I was willing to take more chances to achieve my objectives. I fancied having more friends on my side and finding a smart and beautiful girlfriend for myself.

One of the reasons for my new attitude could have been that I was now approaching the end of my university course. I felt, as long as I was studying, that my mental equilibrium was paramount, and that I should have refrained from any controversy that could have upset it. Now, though, my bachelor's degree was in sight, and I knew just an extraordinary event would have prevented me to achieve this goal.

Another reason was, quite simply, biological. I was getting older, and I needed a stable partner on my side. Until that moment, in fact, I did manage to engage just in short-term relationships. Most of the time, this was due to the fact that, out of loneliness and sexual desire, I used to start affairs with girls I did not fancy for the long period. Once my biological crave was satisfied, I was left with the pitiful duty to break up with them. The women that I really wanted always eluded me. Either they rejected my proposals or—even more painfully—they ended our relationship up.

Summer 1999: the job and the crew

As every year, during the summer, I used to interrupt my studies and take on a job to earn myself some money. I did need to meet new girls too. I thought a job as a bartender would have allowed me to achieve both these two objectives. I remember: I even took on a professional training course in order to provide myself with a better chance to be hired.

Eventually, I did get a position in one of Bologna's most renowned summer's clubs. It was located in the middle of one of its most popular parks. Just what I was looking for.

I remember I settled in pretty quickly in my new workplace. I believe the owner / manager of the club was happy with my performance. Soon my work became my life. My colleagues became my friends. I was spending with them even the little free time I had: the few hours after we closed our bar and the only day-off I had every week.

Summer 1999: the girls

As I was expecting, my new job did allow me to get to know lots of new girls. Many I fancied. Yet, again, the same pattern that I experienced before was repeating itself. The women I really wanted eluded me.

I believe, in their mind, I didn't look a strong enough option. Somehow, they preferred to grant a chance to men that, on paper, had fewer prospects in life than me. This frustrated me enormously.

I was left with the only choice to dare more. I had to try harder to impose my personality.

Summer 1999: trouble in sight

I remember, while we were getting deeper into the Bologna summer, the quality of our clientele was noticeably worsening. This made perfect sense: The students and the middle class flew the city for holidays in August. All that was left during this month were the poor. These were mainly uneducated males that were coming to my bar in the evening after a day of hard labor. Their level of aggressiveness was pretty high.

Several times I found myself facing quite rude people. I struggled to defend myself. I clearly didn't know how to react to them. I wasn't able to diffuse the situation. It looked like my mind could work out just two courses of action: take the offense or fight back head on. I was aware, though, any time I didn't find a way to react to an insult would mean that my reputation among my peers would go lower.

Summer 1999: the win

One evening my frustration reached the breaking point. I don't remember clearly how it happened. I believe there was a man who tried to cut the queue at the till. I must have said something to him. He invited me to get out of the bar and face him. To his and everyone's else surprise, I did just that. He froze when I stood in front of him. I punched him straight in the face. He didn't react. We stared at each other for few seconds.

At first, I was a little bit disheartened, as it didn't look like I caused him any damage. Nevertheless, I probably felt like I made my point. I went back into the bar. He disappeared for a while but returned later and asked to speak with my manager. My boss supported me and sent him away.

His return offered me the chance to look at his face a second time: two purple spots had now appeared on both sides of his nose's bridge. I did hurt him! This made my heart rejoice.

I was victorious for one day and one day only. But I still remember how sweet my feelings were that night. I must have slept deeply for the first time in a long period.

When I came back to work the next day, one of my colleagues looked at me with pride. Beautiful girl with blue eyes! I fancied her deeply. To this day, I still have the image of her admiring glance in my memory.

Summer 1999: the loss

The very following night, I had a second encounter. This time was less successful. It was a weird customer of ours. A man in a struggle, like me. He used to come to our bar late in the evening, just after his work had ended. He was trying his best to find himself a girlfriend. Once, I witnessed him flirting with one of my colleagues with not much success, I have to add. Another time, he froze (or pretended to freeze) when leaning on my bar, his eyes open. I remember I had to shook him to get him to move. He didn't like that.

That evening, I believe, he said something unpleasant to me. I must have been rude back to him, as he challenged me to a fight. I told him I would have engage him after I closed the bar.

When I finished my shift, he was still outside. A lot of people around us. We moved to an open space in the park. He was very conciliatory at that point but, I insisted: I didn't want to see him anymore in my bar. He refused. I attacked. We fell on the grass. I remember: I punched him on the head repeatedly. He was desperate. Somehow his hand reached my face. He dipped his nails in my skin and dragged down. Some people separated us. When we stood up my face was in blood; his wasn't. I was told I was bleeding. I went to the bar's toilet to clean myself up. When I came back in the park he was still there. I got scared. I didn't venture a second attack. We just screamed at each other for a while. Eventually, he left.

Summer 1999: the isolation

I did lose that fight. This was the common opinion of all the bystanders. I agreed with them. I believe the reason why I lost that fight was threefold. First, I was the one who started it; hence, anything short of a clear win had to be accounted for as a loss on my record. Second, I was the physically bigger man. Again, I should have won it with margin in order not to leave any doubt about its outcome. Lastly, I was the one left with marks on my face. His damage (if I inflicted any on him) was not visible. Hence, to all the witnesses, I was the one who came out worst.

That night I didn't sleep as well as the one before. When I woke up, I had a call from my boss's personal assistant telling me I had been fired from my job. She said they needed to take action against an employee who had physically assaulted a costumer. It was either that or the will of the owner to protect me from further fights or, most likely, a combination of the two. I was actually quite relieved by this news; I didn't protest.

Some days later, I came back in the bar for a sort of final farewell. To my surprise everyone was quite cold toward me. These people had been all the friends

I had in the previous few months. Now, it looked like there would be no continuation of our relationship.

Summer 1999: trauma

I remember, after the fight, I remained frozen in my bed for the following two or three days. My head hurt. I was in a state of trauma, and I was conscious of it.

My cell phone stopped ringing. I was deeply concerned for myself and my future. In the months following this accident, even if I couldn't perceive it clearly, I believe my personality changed. I became less secure of myself, more suspicious of what people said or thought. I was more sensitive and tried to react quickly and strongly to any word or action addressed toward me that could be interpreted as hostile.

Overall, I was a less confident and positive man. This, of course, deteriorated the relationship I had with my long-standing friends. Some of them, eventually, deserted me. The ones who didn't cut me off completely made our ties looser.

Summer 1999: my analysis

The pain that I was feeling was immense. As many human beings in similar conditions to mine, I could now rely just on my brain to accurately analyze my current status and seek a way out.

By that time, I had already quite a strong background in several fields of studies. After the initial commotion, my diagnosis of what had happened was quite clear: My defeat on the grass of that park that night was just nature telling me I had been selected.

I was simply not strong enough, not smart enough to achieve my goals.

I had a look around and all seemed clear to me. I could observe how humanity could easily be divided in several categories according to the degree of success each of us had in her or his own life. How it is clear, to all of us, what makes for a "good life," the one we all want to live, and, conversely, how does it look an existence we don't want to be associated with. Also, how early we can guess our destiny and how often we are correct about our predictions. As Noodles said in *Once Upon a Time in America*: "You can always tell the winners at the starting gates."

Summer 1999: genes

Genes. My speculation led me to question my genes. I was aware this was quite a terminal thought. We cannot modify them. We need to go through life with the ones we have got.

At the end of that summer, I was reasoning more or

less in these terms: If the root cause of my failure was my genes, then my life could have been (and would have been) nothing else than a repeating cycle of hopes and disappointments. My final goal, a rich, full existence, one with public recognition by my peers, would have always eluded me.

I understood the rational course of action should have been to kill myself. I pondered: If I were an animal, I would have already been dead by then. Just the fact that I belonged to such a dominant species meant I did not have to pay this high price for my shortfalls.

Summer 1999: suicide

I considered suicide. I was instinctively scared by this idea. It is a jump into the unknown. Furthermore, I knew I would have not been able to kill myself without inflicting a good amount of pain to my body. What if I tried to kill myself and I did only suffer an injury? What if I just created a disability? I would have still been alive, but with even fewer prospects than the ones I had before my attempt.

At the same time, I was building a rational argument against suicide. Why do we take an action? We do it to achieve a result that we would have not reached otherwise. So, why to kill ourselves? Death is an outcome that we cannot miss. We will experience it one day, necessarily. No need to induce it. The only condition that stands as a possibility is our life. I just needed to make sure it had the features I wanted.

Summer 1999: is there a way out?

I had to speculate further. If I did carry on living, I had to have a chance to full happiness. I did not want to settle for anything less.

Maybe my destiny was not written in stone. Maybe it was not true that I had been selected. I thought hard and I came up with three scenarios under which I could still be a winner. I could have been successful in my future if, firstly, I had a better life cycle than my peers; secondly, I did out-develop them; or, lastly, I did change the environment I was in.

I believe, I could have been happy if just one of these three scenarios would have come to fruition. On the other hand, I knew I had to try to pursue the contemporary realization of all three of them in order to maximize my chances of success.

My life's cycle

We are a bundle of skills and muscles that interact every day with the surrounding environment. From the outcome of this relation depends our success in life. We all experience, though, our faculties have not been bestowed upon us in a discreet, immutable amount.

We go through a life cycle. Our capacities grow in our early years, reach a peak in our adulthood, and then progressively decline as we get old.

Because of this evolution in life, we are rarely compared to humanity in general. We are mostly in competition with the individuals of our generation. These are the people we have to prevail upon in order to be successful.

The rate with which our faculties develop and decline varies from human to human. At the peak of its performance, my intelligence may be not as acute as the one of a peer. Yet, if its rate of decline is inferior to the one of my competitors, I will be able to outsmart them in a later stage of life. An individual who is successful in her or his twenties may not achieve the same result in their forties or sixties; and, vice versa.

Of course, I didn't know what would have been my trajectory. It could have been that I would have found myself even more at a disadvantage when I was older. Yet, this possibility did open up my future. This was not bound anymore to repeat the past.

Maximize my potential

Our faculties are not carved into stone. They are not like the functions of a computer that are limited to the software that has been uploaded into it. We are alive. This means our capacities grow and deteriorate. They follow our life cycle. They, also, change according to the care we take of them.

Humans have a separate function that influence all their other ones. Specifically, its job is either to maximize our potential or slow down, as much as possible, our deterioration. It is the brain power that makes us eat healthily, exercise, plan, go to sleep early. It is the one that allow us to learn from the past and change our behavior.

This faculty is a game changer. It doesn't prevent us from losing today if someone else is smarter than us. However, it will allow us to prevail on them in the future by surpassing their development or preservation rate. This faculty is the most human of all our faculties. It is our capacity to develop and maximize all the other ones we have. It has been the one that has allowed us to prevail over all the other animals.

On the 22nd of May 1993, Bernard Hopkins squared off against Roy Jones Jr. in Washington, D.C. He lost. The same two men faced off again on April 3, 2010. This time he won. It happens many times in boxing that fights between the same two men held at different times will yield a different outcome. I like to think this contrast in the results is due to one of the two out-developed or out-preserved the other, either because of his genes or his own capacity to preserve himself.

Changing the environment I was in

The other term in my equation is the environment. Clearly, all our faculties are effective on someone or something. They don't exist or function in isolation. We can assume there is a setting out there for which our present skills, whatever they are, would be just fine. Our only issue, within this scenario, would be to actually live in that environment.

I already hinted how my downfall in the summer of 1999 coincided with a noticeable change in the clientele of our bar. Of course, in our life we need to be able to adapt as, inevitably, we pass through different backgrounds. Simultaneously, though, I think we should aim to make the setting we are most suited for as our main one.

The question that I had to answer, therefore, was: "Within which environment could I be successful?" This, inevitably, led to another query: "What am I good at?" This is kind of awkward, as it always is when you have to describe yourself. I would say I am an educated man, well above the population's average. I am not a quick thinker, but I am able to apply my brain to a particular subject for a long time, always refining my analysis. I believe a highly educated and complex society would have been the one that best suits me.

Of course, this kind of environment is present in

many countries. It was certainly existing in Italy at the time I was making these reflections. However, it is much more widespread in other nations. I am referring specifically to the Nordic ones.

So around that time, I started to consider a change of country. My happiness was at stake, and I had to do everything I could to maximize my chances to grasp it.

SUMMER 2017

The absolute

A law is an absolute. It is like a line drawn on the ground. From that moment onward, everything can be referenced to it. I am either on one or the opposite side of the mark. I am this far from it.

Before the line was drawn, there was no way to identify my position. It could have been argued I was wherever. A law is the opposite of relativism.

The law of natural selection divides us between fit and unfit. It brings absolute in our lives. This clarity cascades down to all the components that make up our success or failure. From our beauty to our intelligence, from our physical performance to our social skills.

This regularity permeates our entire existence. It is how we can establish the winner of an IQ test or a beauty pageant. It is the common reference that provides us with direction and allows the members of our species to evaluate each other's performance.

The introduction of relativism

Our society is permeated with relativism. We always take care to specify we are beautiful, smart, courageous, etc., for someone or a defined group of people. Absolute is a taboo word in our society.

Relativism has been introduced to lower down human conflict. Without its presence, it would be clear who are the winners and the losers. Within this setting, it is easy to expect the latter to constantly rebel until any speck of life is left in her or his body.

Let's assume I marry an unattractive woman. As long as, on a public stage, it is said she is beautiful to me, I will retain a certain degree of strength and success around my persona. If this were not the reality, if it was allowed to publicly speak about my failure to appeal to a beautiful woman, then my weakness would be exposed, and I would be under constant social attack. As a consequence, I would feel inclined to fight back. I would seek a win for myself or—the same to say—somebody's else loss.

What is success?

What is success? In answering this question, it is easy to think about money and power. These are, indeed, means to it, not success itself. What we do with money and power? Quite simply we use them to guarantee our own life. They preserve us from physical labor. They spare us from the anguish to wonder if we will be able to sustain ourselves in the future. They guarantee us the best food and medical care. They ensure we are going to live in salubrious environments. The result is a longer and healthier life. A life in which pain is minimized and we can focus just on the satisfaction of our desires.

On the other hand, preservation of our own life is just the first step toward success. We cannot think ourselves as a single existence. If we do that, we would have to acknowledge the reward for our life's effort would be pretty limited. We think big. We think of ourselves as part of a *gens*. A stream of similar selves that run across history. We want to protect and expand this flow. We want it to carry on for as far as possible into the future. We want children and we want to make sure they will be able to further pass on our genes. We are going to use our money and power to protect and reinforce not just us, but our lineage too.

Recently, I read a newspaper article about brothers Charles and David Koch from Kansas in Unites States. They are a couple of octogenarian businessmen with a present estimated wealth of 50 billion dollars each. This is much more that they will be able to spend in what is left of their lives. Despite this, they are currently fighting tooth and nail any increase of the federal minimum wage, fixed at $7.25 per hour. They are not mad.

This makes perfect sense. They understand any cent they earn or save will further extend the protection around their lineage into the future.

Time: the healer

The summer of 1999 has been a turning point in my life. An adjustment for the worst, obviously. I already mentioned how, after it, I entered a vicious circle of bad temper-loss of friends-bad temper. It really seemed for some time an unstoppable spiral. Yet, something changed over time. The freefall slowed down. Eventually, it stopped to a new balance. A different quality of life began for me that was somewhat inferior to the already unsatisfactory one I had before.

While I was recovering, I tried as much as I could to avoid confrontation. Every clash we engage in bears a consequential effect on us: Either we win and boost ourselves, or we lose and weaken our confidence. Dodging confrontation enabled me to feel like I was not losing anymore, at least not noticeably. For each skirmish I was giving up, I could still trick myself into thinking I would have won if I cared enough to fight.

Time is not neutral. Time cured me. Our mind heals from its wounds just as our body does with its. Cowardly, we forget or blur our shames. With time, my self-confidence returned. Until, I was finally ready to mount another charge.

The conclusion of my experience in Italy

In the year 2000, I managed to prepare and pass just two exams at university. The year 2001 was the one of my bachelor's degree. I was 29 by then. Between this year and 2004, I studied to gain a teacher's training certificate. My subjects were history and philosophy. I would have taught to students in high school.

I managed to pass all my exams and prepare my thesis. Yet, somehow, I was cracking under pressure. I was growing impatient with my situation. I wanted to become independent and autonomous. I felt a strong psychological strain to be better of what I was. I knew it was long overdue for me to stand on my own feet. Society was asking me for that, and I was getting tired to play coy to justify my current status.

In February 2004, I left Italy for the first time. It was a weekend in London. The fresh air was stinging my skin. I moved there the following August.

Why England

The root of my decision to move to United Kingdom lies firmly in the reflection I made in the summer of 1999. Ideally, I would have wanted to relocate to one of the Nordic countries. I was just dreaming about the high level of education and the good quality of life the people of those societies enjoy. However, I never studied any of their languages in school. This made any prospect to move there quite problematic.

During my upbringing, I studied English, as most Italians do. Across the turn of the century, many of my country's people had already moved to United Kingdom, attracted by its rich and dynamic job market.

I came across the British culture several times during my education. I studied their history, philosophy, and literature. I had the privilege to watch their movies and comedies. The idea that I formed in my mind was the one of a society much more developed and refined of the Italian one.

For instance, on Italian television, we never had a show that matched the quality of *Monty Python's Flying Circus*. Not even by the time I left my country. Italian comedy was mainly slapstick and a teasing of regional stereotypes. Monty Python, on the other hand, had been groundbreaking both in its format and content. Its sketches often include references to important historical events and personalities. On some occasions, their skits would involve a deep criticism of modern society. The hollowness of popular conceptions was exposed. Metaphysical ideas concerning the absurdity of life, or the absence of any firmly rooted morality, were continuously hinted at.

The same disparaging comparison can be also made between the two literatures. Whereas in the previous two centuries, Italian authors had been unable to deal with the aftermath of progress and modernization in any other way than self-lamenting and condemnation, their English counterparts had risen to the challenge of conceptually understanding these ideas of progress and modernization as well as outlining a new ethics fitting to contemporary society.

Ultimately, in my mind, there was no doubt Great Britain would have made a much more suitable background to my life than Italy.

Welcome to London

My arrival in the United Kingdom coincided with a complete reset of my state of mind. Nobody knew me here; there were no expectations about my persona. My Italian life's plan, with its schedule to abide to, had been obliterated overnight. I felt much more relaxed. In Italy, I was relying on pills to sleep. In my new country, I started again to rest naturally.

I loved London since the beginning. I was enchanted by the magnificence of its buildings, both classic and contemporary. Yet, what filled me with enthusiasm was probably not just their beauty. It was what their grandness stood for: The vast wealth that the city was holding and that I, now, had a chance to participate in.

I could see a lot of people owned homes. Restaurants and cinema were full. Large green areas.

Museums and art galleries open and free to everyone. Lovely pathways regularly maintained. It was like the middle class did manage to force the rich to share part of their prosperity. The result was that a good life looked like an easy reach here in London.

On the top of this, British society looked to me much more structured than the Italian one. It seemed like, for any purpose or objective you were setting to yourself, there was a clear path in front of you. Nobody was doing your job for you, but all the information, advice, materials, institutions, you may have needed in order to accomplish it were, in fact, available to you.

British people didn't disappoint me either. They were well educated and articulate as I expected them to be. Quite truly, it was refreshing to watch on television common people being able to discuss rationally political or cultural subjects. It was nice to see everyone taking particular care to logically connect the terms of their own argument and detect for themselves the limits of its validity.

Fairly soon, moving to United Kingdom, felt like coming home to me. Quite a beautiful sensation to experience.

My life in the United Kingdom

In this country, I started what can be called an "active" life, especially if I compare it to the one I was conducting in Italy. I began to work regularly. This helped me to discharge my brain. I was happy to be engaged with day-to-day issues and not with complex and abstract speculations as I used to be during my studies. As a result of this new lifestyle, I shed some weight. I started to look fitter, and my overall appearance improved.

At the beginning of my experience in Britain, I did all sorts of manual jobs. I needed it in order to sustain myself. In the meanwhile, I constantly enhanced and improved my English. Quite soon, I could apply for public-facing jobs. Later, I started a career in accounting. By 2014, I had reached a management position within this field.

In 2015, I purchased an apartment. I did it with the assistance of the government's "Help to Buy" scheme. This brought much more stability into my life. At the same time, though, it committed me to an onerous repayment plan.

My career

Looking at my career from afar, it could have appeared I was very successful. I did start it doing unskilled manual jobs. It progressed to the point I reached a management position in a professional occupation. My income was above the national average for my role.

The reality, though, was another. My career had

not been a straight line. Quite a series of accelerations and setbacks. The way I see it, I was propped up by my competency, skills, and hard work. However, I felt held back in terms of my interpersonal skills. As such, I had to watch colleagues with a fraction of my capacities go up the career ladder in front of me.

Interpersonal and communication skills are key for our success not just in our private life, but, also, in our career. Of course, nobody can advance in his profession on their base alone. As well, a lot of their incidence will depend on the kind of manager we work for. Nonetheless, it is undeniable: Interpersonal and communication skills are important assets to have. They will always work as an amplifier of our professional capacities or a blur to our limitations.

Ms. S.

I met Ms. S. on a Tuesday evening in November 2016. We actually came across each other on an internet dating site. I should say at the outset that I didn't go to this date with any higher expectation than I had for previous ones.

By the time I met Ms. S., I had been through a lot of meetups. What I learned was that their outcome was quite unpredictable: I found myself getting along with women who had very different profiles. Because of this, I preferred to apply just a basic screening (centered on appearance and relationship's objectives) of the women I was contacting. This had led me to send a lot of invitations out such that I opted to create a standard format for my opening text. Here it is:

Hi [],

I believe you have a beautiful face and I like your profile.

Please have a look at mine.

Would you like to tell me something more about yourself?

Ciao

Xxx

The only original part in my messages would have been, if available, the name of the woman.

Ms. S. looked very beautiful and fit in her pictures. Her self-presentation seemed pretty standard to me. I believe she mentioned she had her own career; she loved the countryside and to travel. She was divorced and had a son, as is the case for many women her age. Nothing anyway that, at that point, made her stand out from other profiles I was looking at.

The date

I met her just outside my work place. As soon as she realized I was her date, she had an expression of disappointment on her face. I believe I must have not looked as good as in my pictures.

We went to a nearby coffee shop and talked. Her appearance did not disappoint: her face was incredibly beautiful, with an elegant quality about her. She had dark hair. She was tall with a slim body.

I believe, at the beginning, we had quite a plain conversation, just feeding each other the basic information concerning our lives. Later on, we expanded it to our likes, plans, and even current affairs. As in similar meetings, I tried to make witty remarks to impress my counterpart. However, she didn't react to them.

Generally speaking, our first talk was nothing special. What was good about it, though, was that it did flow. By the end of it, I was pleasantly surprised to notice she was showing a good disposition toward myself. I believe, after the first hiccup, she started to like my appearance. I reckon she was also charmed by the calm and articulate manner with which I expressed myself. Above all, it looked like what mattered to her was for me to meet some basic requirements she had already set in her mind. She was not looking for me to stand out in any particular way—at least not at that moment.

From my side, apart from her appearance, I was impressed by her maturity and rational thinking. It was nice to see she was willing to talk about just everything I touched upon during our conversation.

At the end of our meeting, I didn't have any doubt about asking her for a second date.

Humor and human intelligence

I've always held humor in high regard among all the human faculties. To me, it is a clear sign of intelligence. I still remember from the movie *Quest for Fire* by Jean-Jacques Annaud (1981), how the capacity to laugh at an apple falling on someone's head was considered as much a mark of a more evolved society as the mastering of fire or frontal sex.

What is genius? I believe the correct answer to this question is the ability to find a link between terms that appear to be completely unrelated one to the other. Further is the distance between the areas they belong to, the bigger the intelligence necessary to establish an association between them must be.

The theory of relativity explains why the speed of light does not change with the movement of the observer. Albert Einstein achieves this result through the intuition that space and time are variable dimensions. He establishes this connection in contradiction both to common perception and classical physics.

Now, let's examine a random joke: "Relationships are like fat people... Most of them don't work out." The laughter in this pun sparks by the close pairing of two ideas that, at a first glance, appear to be completely unrelated one to the other: a feeling between humans, on one side; a group of people identified by a physical character, on the other. The author of this joke obtains this result through the insight both these concepts are often used in association with the same verb, "work out," albeit it assumes a completely different acceptation when combined with each of the two.

Our relationship progresses

I kissed Ms. S. the following Saturday. A few weeks later, after her son had reached his father for early Christmas holidays, we had sex. Sex with Ms. S. was very exciting and, therefore, gratifying. She had a very attractive body; she enjoyed it and she was always very attentive to her man's needs.

We went for a weekend away. Then, we briefly separated for our Christmas holidays. We resumed our meetings in January.

At this point our conversation was pretty fluid. It looked like we were both happy with each other and we were seeing a future together. We were talking about having children of our own.

We both agreed the first action to take to move our relationship forward was to introduce myself to her son. Following this, I would move in with them, and through this we would further test our compatibility.

Economic wellness and stability

Of course, not all was going well. The first time I distinctly detected an issue between us was when she told me how much she was earning. This was between three and four times what I was paid. She followed this up by letting me know how, ideally, she was expecting her man to make double her income. Her objective was to conduct a quality life. She was dreaming about a large house in the countryside. She didn't like the noise and confusion of the big city. She once surprised me quoting some data about the poor air quality of London. I found her concern a bit exaggerated, as I knew our city didn't compare unfavorably to other European capitals. On the other hand, I couldn't help but admire her intelligence in focusing on such a critical indicator and discarding many other ones commonly used when sizing up a city.

In substance, she wanted an upper-middle-class life. Financial solidity. Periodic holidays to explore the world. Enough money to send our children to the best schools so that our lineage could prosper in the long run.

I didn't agree with her in linking so closely wealth and happiness. However, I did find her aspiration for economic stability legitimate.

Why isn't the telephone ringing?

Another piece of her ideal life was being part of a substantial network of friends. A group of peers to share experience with, to communicate with, to feel protected by.

Also, about this aspiration I could not advance any exceptions.

I remember one time when we went out for a walk in the park close to her place. All of a sudden, she turned toward me and asked, "Why does your phone never ring?" She caught me by surprise on this one. I looked at her speechless for few seconds. One part of me was embarrassed by the substance of her question: I knew I should have had more friends. Another side of me noticed its peculiar delivery: She must have lingered on this thought for some time before that moment. She was expecting a fitting explanation.

I told her that some of the friends I made over my time in London had left the city. Others got married, and so they now had a different life routine compared to mine. I believe I also hinted on the fact that it was more difficult to make friends at my age than it was in my twenties. I reassured her I was still planning to make new ones. At that moment, she appeared to be satisfied by my answer.

My manager's birthday party

I didn't assign to the above hints the correct weight. As far as I was concerned, I was in a solid relationship. Ms. S. and I had quite a dense schedule for the months to come and she was still very careful to involve me in any long-term decision.

At the beginning of March 2017 my manager's birthday party came up. He invited me. It was a simple Saturday afternoon barbeque at his home. It was also my occasion to show Ms. S. that I was capable of some sociality.

After a brief introduction we sat with other friends by a table in the garden, with Ms. S. on my side. We just started a conversation. My manager was busy preparing the appetizers in the kitchen. My girlfriend, quite abruptly, stood up and went to join him. She didn't say a word to me. I could not see them. At the table there were two of my colleagues. In their eyes, I could see their surprise. They knew the two were strangers to each other. Nobody uttered a word about it though.

Her body language was of a woman looking to entice a man.

Heart racing

My heart started racing inside my chest. I was still trying to hold a part in the table's conversation while my mind was desperately attempting to compute what did just materialize.

Could this action by Ms. S. be interpreted in any other way than her opening a door to my manager? Could this be the action of a person that, considering herself in a solid relationship, felt free to meet new people without expecting her partner to be jealous? If that was the case, she would have been quite reckless, as these types of deeds are deemed to upset and hurt a partner no matter how much you rationalized them.

Was she testing me? Did she want to find out how I would have reacted in a difficult situation? Maybe.

Still the best explanation for her action was that she was a woman unsatisfied with her current relationship and on the lookout to find a new and better one.

Ironically, some days earlier, when I asked my manager if I could bring my girlfriend with me at his party, he made a joke in front of the whole office about him stealing her from me. I laughed at his joke. I deemed him too old and unattractive to be a competitor of mine. Now, though, while she was still talking with him in the kitchen, I remembered her saying to me she was not focused on her partner's physical appearance. Her priorities were for her companion to have a large circle of friends and a solid economic position. Even more ironic, once she impatiently pressured me to estimate how long it would have taken me to be promoted to my manager's position.

Because of all these considerations, I had now to change my original assessment of my manager: He was, indeed, a contender of mine. I had to defend myself.

No action

My first instinct was to rush into the kitchen and punch my opponent straight in his face. I reasoned, though, that would have not made much sense. After all, he wasn't guilty of anything. I thought about storming into the kitchen and taking her away with me. However, that would have been quite a terminal action to undertake. It would have amounted to admitting she was doing something wrong. What if that wasn't true? What if there was another explanation for her behavior?

My mind was reeling. I couldn't put my thoughts in a clear order. Overall, though, I felt that what was going on was unacceptable. Eventually, I deemed the right course of action would have been to break up with Ms. S. on the way back home.

After several minutes that felt like an eternity to me, she came back from the kitchen. Later, I saw my manager too. He couldn't look into my eyes and he had a very apologetic tone any time he addressed me. The group had some social moments, then we sat and ate. Ms. S. and I left early because she didn't want to leave her young son alone for too long.

On our way back, a lot was going on in my mind but, somehow, I didn't find words good enough to express it. I remained mostly silent. She knew something was stirring up inside me. She preferred not to investigate, though. She spoke of the party like everything that went on in it was totally normal and average.

New status

When I first approached love many years ago, I thought that tenderness and kindness would have been the only legitimate attitude toward my partner. With time I understood that this is not the case. As I mentioned in relation to friendship: We want to be associated with a strong ally. A weak partner is just a weight, eventually. We have to be sturdy, and we have to demonstrate our strength to our companion each day.

What happened at the party had changed the complexion of our relationship. In my mind, her action was her way to communicate to me she was not happy with it. It was a warning addressed to me. I knew, if I had not done anything, that it would have meant I was accepting this new state of uncertainty.

I had to strike back. I had to let her know I did not agree with her behavior. That I was ready to break up our relationship if it was not the loving and caring one I wanted. I just needed to find the right occasion to express my thoughts.

Our first argument

It occurred just few weeks after the party. We went out for our traditional after-dinner walk. I don't remember exactly what she said, but it was a remark of dissatisfaction toward me. I faced her head on. "You don't need to be with me. It is not an instruction from your doctor. You either are with me because you respect and love me, or we can end this now."

In my heart I was ready for that to be last night of our relationship. Considering her attitude in the previous days, I was not expecting her to fight for it. Yet, she did. I could see a sense of fear in her eyes. Maybe she didn't want to be the cause again for another of her relationships to end.

I pick up some stuff I had at her place, and I went to the bus stop. She follows me. I stop her. I ask her to think about us before to come back to me. I tell her I want a break. We need a pause to reflect. We should be back together just if we are completely sure this is what we want. She follows me at the bus stop and then on the bus. She tells me how good our sex is. That was the only argument I remember she made in favor of our relationship.

When we are approaching the tube station, I deemed that she did enough to prove she cares about me and wanted to be with me. I hug her tight. We go back to her place.

The bliss

With the boldness of that evening, I had temporarily reestablished myself as a valuable partner on her side. My reward was a period of bliss that lasted a few weeks.

On the weekdays, I was pretty busy with my work. In the evenings, I was often sleeping at Ms. S.'s place and always on the weekends.

After dinner we were frequently playing some card or board games. Her child, a teenager of 14, was very competitive and passionate about them. Ms. S. told me at one point she looked at my performance in those games as a measure of my intelligence.

Over the weekends I was usually struggling. I had few close friends, but I deemed none of them were a match for the personality and culture of Ms. S. The lack of peers meant our weekends missed this important element of variety and enrichment. Overall, it made our relationship weaker. I managed, though, to organize some one-day trips with her and her son. We went to see some of London's attractions such as the Shard and the Olympic Village. We went to Cambridge on a Sunday.

In relation to my own career, I was now determined to finish the accounting qualification I started. I was often dedicating Saturday and Sunday mornings to its study.

During the spring I started again to run in the park.

I had to interrupt this, though, as I was hampered by quite a pernicious tendinitis.

Ms. S.'s aspirations

We need to earn our respect every day in life. This is little but sure.

It looks to me in those months I must have failed to achieve this objective with Ms. S. and her son. Hence, I have been excluded from their life.

I believe Ms. S.'s ideal man would have been a successful professional in his forties. The expression "successful professional" implies this man had the following two characteristics. First, he must be smart to learn a profession and to go further in his career than others. Second, he was wealthy or could count on a large income.

Ms. S. also wanted her man to have social skills. With it she meant he had to have charisma and be able to hold his own in social gatherings. He had to appear strong to his peers, so that a vast group of people would have sought his friendship and a thick, protective circle would have been formed around him.

As already mentioned, his appearance was not a priority but within certain limits. Of course, it would have been a welcomed extra if he was handsome too.

Intelligence, skills, wealth, a vast circle of friends. In my mind, all of this was adding up to the same objective: security. This was what Ms. S. was after. This is what every living being is after according to the law of natural selection.

The discrepancy

I have something in common with Ms. S.'s ideal man. This was the reason why we got together in the first place. I was, indeed, a professional in my forties. I did make a career over the years, so much so that by the time I met her, I was holding a management's position.

However, at a closer look, my success was not good as it could have appeared. In my career, I didn't progress as far as I could and should have. I was not making a good amount of money, especially if considered I didn't own any substantial assets. I didn't manage to secure a circle of successful friends around myself. You could just foresee it: I would have been in severe financial difficulties if I had lost my job.

I believe, over time, Ms. S. evaluated my position more and more as weak and precarious. This was not what she wanted.

The inner conflict

I reckon that Ms. S. became progressively aware of the discrepancy between what she was expecting from her man and what I could offer her. She must have been conflicted about what action to take for some time. During this period, a feeling of concern was growing into her.

The way she was expressing her dissatisfaction was not direct. She was either not completely conscious of what she didn't like about me, or she simply didn't feel like to speak to me openly. She preferred to communicate through little actions that she knew would have hurt me. For instance, she may have not waited for me for dinner or expressed a remark any time I made an error, no matter how little it was.

By this time, I was deeply fond of Ms. S. I would have dearly loved for her to remain on my side. Yet, I knew there was no point for me to concede to her annoyances. If I would have done that, her consideration of me would have sunk even lower and I would have had yet slimmer chances to continue our relationship.

Ms. S. leaves me

We had another argument in May. I left her. She came back to me. This time without the same urgency.

Then, another one in June. It came at the end of a particular intense period of her irritations. I left her a final time. She didn't do anything to stop me on this occasion. Actually, it looked like she was just waiting for this to happen. The first time I broke up with her, I asked her to hand me over the keys of my apartment.

She could not find them back then. This time they were on display on her bedroom's desk.

Her mind was clearly made up. She quickly organized for my possessions to be sent back to my property. I did not hear from her again.

Who was Ms. S.? - part one

Ms. S. was a 40-year-old woman hailing from Russia. I believe the crucial point in her life was the time when she split up with her husband. This happened in her early thirties.

Ms. S. is a natural beauty. She is also a very smart person. She met her future husband at university. They were both studying software engineering. I believe a lot of people within this profession think of themselves as very smart. This must be because the complexity of the subject they master prevents a lot of students even to attempt this academic course. Among the ones who join it, many drop out before completing their studies. I would have not been surprised if, between the few ones that make it to the end, many of them think of themselves as a sort of selected elite.

Graduates in software engineering tend to be in great demand in the workforce. For this reason, they are often rewarded for their efforts with a very high salary.

I guess economic wellness and security at such young age raise your expectations and make you very demanding. I don't know exactly how it started, but something happened in their marriage that made Ms. S. feel neglected. She is a woman who is neither modest nor patient. As such, she took action that humiliated her husband. She did that not because she stopped loving him. She did it just to hurt him and remind him of how precious and important she was. Ms. S. flunked her calculation. Her husband did not put up with the humiliation and quickly went on to form a new family with another woman.

I believe until that moment Ms. S. was convinced her life would have turned out as an easy fairy tale. She never contemplated the possibility of a failure. Now, though, she was a divorced single mum in her thirties. Her financial situation was not secure. She had just lost a very smart and successful man. Above anything else, the sinking feeling she had brought all of this upon herself through her own mistake.

Who was Ms. S.? - part two

When Ms. S. spoke to me about this period of her life, I understood she suffered a psychological trauma. She went through a lot of pain.

However, the thing about Ms. S. is that she is extremely smart. It was because of her intelligence that she was a software engineer at 21. Her brain came to her rescue one more time when she was plunged into this negative situation. She got a hold of herself, and she devised a plan to claw back her objectives within both her finances and personal life.

She started to manage her income and expenses very strictly. In relation to her career, she proceeded to identify the best jobs she could aspire to. She worked meticulously to have all the credentials necessary to be successful in her applications. She made sure she had a good employment record. She reviewed her CV in every little detail. She thoroughly prepared for her interviews. She cultivated a network of professional references within her industry. Eventually, she landed a very high-paying job in a well-known multinational corporation based in London.

Regarding her private life, Ms. S. was too clever to be distracted by the hypocrisy of society. She knew men are attracted by a woman's appearance. For this reason, and even though she was already good looking, she proceeded to improve herself. She started to exercise regularly. She paid more attention to what she was wearing.

Ms. S. also understood how important sex is for a man. For this reason, she was very attentive to please her partners in this area too.

I believe, after what happened with her ex-husband,

she was determined to make sure no other man would have ever left her.

After her divorce, she started a long-term relationship with another software engineer. This got interrupted by her moving to London. In this city she started a number of liaisons that didn't last very long. The one she had with me was one of them.

Why I loved Ms. S.

I loved Ms. S. for the same reason why anyone loves anybody else on this Earth: because I think she is a winner. I reckon I hold this opinion because of her cleverness, her physical appearance, her determination, and her confidence.

One of the imagines I have got of Ms. S. is her playing brain teasers on her way to work. She told me she did it to sharpen her intelligence. I was enchanted by her competitiveness.

I had been meeting a lot of women in my life by this time. With most of them I was unsure about our prospects. I was always asking them out one more time, hoping that date would have been the litmus test that would have cleared out my mind. Ms. S. belonged to a restricted group of women I had no doubt about since almost the beginning of our relationship. I was sure I wanted to marry her and to form a family with her.

The break-up: its effects on me

I believe I managed to maintain my composure in front of Ms. S. when we split. I cried and sobbed when I returned home and for a certain time after then. I was suffering a psychological trauma, once again, in my life. Such was the pain I was feeling.

I reckon: It is normal to ache any time we lose somebody we love. In my case, though, there was nothing to sweeten my pill. First of all, this was not a consensual break-up. It was her decision. A choice that stemmed, quite simply, from her acknowledgment she didn't feel happy with me. Furthermore, I couldn't even claim she didn't know me well enough. We had been together for six months. We used to lie together. We woke up together. Hers was an informed decision.

As in the summer of 1999, when I picked myself up from that grass in the middle of a park in Bologna, it was like nature was telling me I wasn't good enough. This was my essence. Even if I was going to find another partner in my life as good as Ms. S., she would eventually leave me, as I would have not been able to make her happy.

What is trauma?

I often think of our consciousness as a landscape. Our experiences are the weather that molds it. Sometimes it is mild and nurtures the scenery; sometimes it is dreadful and wrecks it. A trauma is a deep uneven mark that the weather has left on our landscape.

As in the case of human consciousness, time eventually smooths out our scars. Trees die. The wind brings dust. A new layer of terrain covers the old one. New landscapes stand on the previous ones. Because of this, each new layer resembles the preceding one; it is, indeed, a more rounded and docile version of the previous one.

In a landscape, as in our conscience, the outer layer is mainly determined by the second layer. This, in turn, is influenced by the previous one. And so on, one after the other, until the very first level. In our mind, no experience is completely forgotten.

A severe dent will be visible on the terrain over several layers. Yet, eventually, provided we will not permit the weather to aggravate it further, it will disappear. Our landscape will recover some form of harmony.

"Get busy living"

"In life you get busy living or you get busy dying." This is what Andy Dufresne said to Red in *The Shawshank Redemption*. This sentence said *en passant* in a mainstream movie is the pinnacle of our civilization.

"Living." The broad nature of this verb is staggering! "Living." He does not say: "Get busy fighting for what is right" or "realizing your dreams," or, simply, "making a career." He just says: "living." It implies any metaphysic, any absolute, have been obliterated from our horizon. There is no qualitative hierarchy between the actions we can take. They are all equivalent. Even the termination of ourselves.

The only two options between which our reason can still detect a substantial difference are "getting busy" or "not getting busy." This dilemma is solved through mere practicality. Life is a flow of events. To remain idle would condemn us to a state of neglect and suffering. We have to "get busy" to relieve our pain either by ending our existence or pursuing objectives the vacuity of which we are well conscious about.

My decision

In the summer of 2017, I found myself in a similar situation to the one I had suffered in the summer of 1999. I was put in front, one more time, to a massive frustration of my aspirations.

This occurrence didn't surprise me. After what happened in the past, it was, in a way, in my cards. I knew, if I didn't up my game, I would inevitably fail to achieve my objectives, with all the pain and the suffering that result would have carried.

Probably the only difference from 1999 was that this time the entire process of analysis of my current situation and elaboration of a long-term strategy proceeded at a much faster pace. In fact, it appeared to me there was nothing wrong with my life plan. I just needed to be more effective in its implementation. I had to be sharper in my day-to-day decisions, more resolute in following them through. I needed to yield more from myself in order to realize my goals.

Being strong socially

When an animal is wounded it seeks shelter. We, humans, do the same. If we are sick, we stay at home. If we need to go out when we are ill, we dress to look healthy. We hide our weaknesses. We pretend to be what we are not.

We do this because, intimately, we know we are locked in a struggle between each other. The moment in which we are vulnerable is the occasion for our competitors to pounce on us.

When somebody leaves us, they weaken us. This is because such a gesture implies the leaver doesn't think we are winners. If she or he did so, they would have felt secure and happy with us. Hence, they would have not abandoned us.

I knew Ms. S. leaving was making me more vulnerable in front of my peers. On the other hand, I didn't want to pretend. I felt I didn't have anything to hide. So that, to whoever was asking, I candidly replied that she left me. I was determined, however, not to accept any attack or innuendo addressed to myself in case they did arise.

Is she with my manager?

At the time Ms. S. left me, I thought it could be the case she found another man. In fact, her change of attitude toward me had been surprisingly sharp. All of a sudden, she looked very convinced and resolute that I was not the man for her. She lacked the hesitation that normally comes upon us any time we face the prospect of being alone again.

Maybe she found another man in her workplace. Maybe she met somebody on the train. Maybe she was now with my manager. As soon as this thought entered my mind, I fell in a state of deep discomfort. I was frightened, terrified by this prospect. The humiliation that such a situation would bring me would have been immense and impossible to bear.

From a rational point of view, I was aware that it didn't really matter who she was with after leaving me. What was important was that the woman I loved left me. That she did not feel happy with me. That she was no longer at my side when I was waking up. That she would no longer look at me with a smile.

Yet the idea she was with my manager still horrified me. I tried to understand why.

Dissection of a humiliation

I reckon the reason why I would have felt particularly humiliated to lose out to my manager was that I didn't think of him as a strong competitor. He was older, less attractive, and in worst physical shape than I was. I didn't hold his intelligence to any particular consideration. He was alone at 52, never married, and, I can say with a certain confidence, with not many female prospects in front of himself. To come in second after him would have implied to me and all my peers that my strengths and capacities were even inferior to his.

It is always important to understand to whom we lose out in our lives. It establishes our public value and the level of competition we are in. For this reason, we find it easier to accept a defeat if the high skills of our opponent are commonly recognized.

I still remember how surprised I was to hear Eddie Irvine publicly acknowledging Michael Schumacher was a faster driver than him. This is such a rare admission between racers. And how quickly he was to specify this concession was limited just to him. Any other competitor being, at best, at an equal level to his.

Of course, another reason why the possibility of Ms. S. and my manager being a couple was very painful to me was that, inevitably, I would have had to see them together in the future. Actually, I would have seen them together every day from then onwards, just across the office, in the happy face of my manager. His smile being the daily reminder of my failure.

A social convention: don't engage romantically with your friend's ex-girlfriend

Once, when I was young, I watched an American TV movie in which one of the characters was asking a friend permission to invite his ex-girlfriend out. I remember I found that request quite petty. First of all, it made it look like someone can still claim to have rights on another person even when they are not engaged in a relationship any longer. Secondly, it caused the asker to appear like a coward, as he was potentially ready to suppress his feelings if another man demanded him to.

Later in my life, I understood that this human practice, as any other one, has a rational reason for its existence. Its purpose is to prevent a social conflict. If we ask someone else for their permission, we achieve two results: First, we acknowledge the existence of the other person as well as of their right to be happy; second, we admit we are weary of the kind of reaction that the person can display. Asking for permission elevates our competitor. This, in turn, will mitigate the humiliation the person is about to suffer. Possibly, this is going to be enough to prevent this person from fighting our action.

The likelihood they were together

What were the chances they were together? As far as I was aware, Ms. S. and my manager met just in two occasions: at the latter's birthday party and at my birthday party. I believe they didn't exchange their contact details on both these events. Yet, as they knew each other's name and place of work, they would have easily been able to find one another on social media.

Therefore, again, it would all come down to if they *wanted* to be together. I believe we can all agree: It is more likely for two individuals to end up together if they yearn for each other at the opposite side of the globe than for two roommates indifferent to one another.

Did Ms. S. want to be with my manager? My mind tries to find any excuse to deny this possibility. He is too old; he is unattractive. The fact of the matter is that he is an educated man and has a solid professional position. Even more important, she made the first move to get to know him at his birthday party. That gesture can hardly be interpreted in any other way than an expression of interest.

In relation to my manager, I had no doubt he wanted to be with her. I could see it in his eyes when he looked at her. I knew how envious he was to see me with such a beautiful and accomplished woman.

He had been a single man for a while by that time.

Few months before, when he split up with his last girlfriend, in a moment of unsettlement, he confessed to me how upset he was she left him. Few days later, after regaining his composure, he retracted his version and boasted he was the one who left her.

On a day-to-day basis, his personality was pretty cheerful. He was always up for some banter. Yet, behind the façade, I could not help but think how lonely he must have felt. Because of his age and appearance, I knew he didn't have many prospects in front of him. None, anyway, of the beauty and intelligence of Ms. S. To me it was a sure thing. I knew he would have proceeded to pursue her now that she was no longer with me.

Would he tell me?

I used to ponder if he would have told me. He knew my feelings for Ms. S. It would have been the respectful thing to do to inform me if something had struck up between the two of them.

I also considered the personality of my manager. A part of me was led to think he was the kind of man who would have made me aware if something did happen between him and my ex-girlfriend. Certainly, he would have felt the moral obligation to do so. Yet, I could not help but thinking he may have not followed through on this initial inclination.

He was a man that was afraid of confrontation. Hence, his brain would have been led to find numerous excuses not to inform me, at least at this stage. He might have thought there was no reason for him to notify me a relationship had started between the two of them as long as it was in its initial stages. He would have eventually communicated this to me just if it grew to be something more solid and meaningful. Alternatively, he could have decided not to warn me to protect me, not to hurt me. Finally, he could have simply deemed we had never been that close friends for him to feel any obligation toward me.

I suspect she's with my manager

I was going to work with a huge knot in my throat. I was just terrified she was now with my manager. I couldn't stop imagining them together. Her being finally happy in his arms.

I was thinking about my colleagues. How could I bear their judgment if such a thing was, in fact, happening?

I was desperate to know if anything was going on. I had my senses heightened to their maximum. I was looking around for signs that would have revealed if anything in my manager's private life had changed.

My anxiety reached paroxysm anytime he was closing his office's door to have a private conversation or, simply, he was lowering his voice, so that I could not hear what he was discussing. From a rational point of view, I knew he was probably debating work matters but somehow, I could not bring myself to calm down.

In the evening, at home, I looked through their profiles in various social networks for evidence either to support or reject my hypothesis.

As I could not find any new information, my uneasiness grew even further. I deemed to take action. One of my neighbors had organized a party in his own apartment on a Saturday afternoon and he invited me to it. I decided to ask my manager if he wanted to join me. I thought that if he was still a single man, he would have picked up my offer as it would have been a good occasion for him to meet new women. To my surprise, he accepted my invitation.

"Are you with my ex-girlfriend?"

At this point I knew that, unfortunately, my little test had not proven anything. It could have been that he didn't have plans to see Ms. S. that particular afternoon. Maybe they already had agreed to see each other just on Sunday over that weekend. Or, more simply, she was not even in London on that day.

I decided to take my action further and ask him directly if he was with my ex-girlfriend. The fact that he was going to come to my place, and we would have had some time alone, would have certainly facilitated my task.

On that Saturday, indeed, he came to my apartment for a drink before to join my neighbor's party. We sit on the sofa. I looked into his eyes and asked him: "Did you try to contact my ex-girlfriend?"

He looked pretty surprised by my question. He hesitated a moment. Then, he answered that he didn't. Somehow, he felt the need to support his statement with rational arguments. He said that, even if he wanted to, he could have not contacted her, as he didn't have her telephone number. He then ended his remarks by simply affirming he was not interested in her.

In my mind, this last statement was a plain lie. I raised my eyebrows to it; however, I did not argue with him. I thought I should have felt already satisfied by his answer.

We finished our drinks and subsequently joined the party.

Some days later, while I was browsing the dating site in which I first met Ms. S., I saw her profile active again. A feeling of deep sorrow caught my heart. I was just witnessing her unwillingly going back to that website in order to find a man able to provide her with that security and happiness I failed to deliver to her.

On the other hand, the fact she was back on that service, did prove to me she was not with anyone at that moment.

Who was my manager?

My manager was a 52-year-old man hailing from Germany. He used to work for a company that would later become our parent. At the time of the acquisition, his manager asked him if he was interested to join the accounting team of the new subsidiary. He was offered a management position within it, but he would have not overseen the entire department. At the time I met him, my manager tried to sell this proposal from his superior as an expression of trust in his capacities. I could not help but feeling, it was the exact opposite. In my mind, in fact, a boss usually tries to retain the services of her or his best employees.

At the beginning of our professional collaboration, I was pretty surprised by his conduct. His behavior was very different from the one of managers I previously worked for. He allowed me and anyone else in the team complete freedom in our initiative. He was not interested in closely supervising our work. Whenever he could, he was keen to delegate his tasks. He was mainly focused on carrying out a core number of duties he felt were strictly related to his position; he was happy to play a supporting role for all other matters concerning the team.

He used to deal with his staff with warmth and graciousness. As basic inclination, he was ready to second all our requests. Between staff and business needs, he tried to favor the former as much as he could. Needless to say, his general attitude made him a very popular boss.

After work, it was his habit to stop by at the local pub. I used to join him time to time. He was able to hold a conversation about a wide range of subjects. He was not interested into sports. He had developed a curiosity for a more refined culture and a vast array of subjects. He often went to theaters and cinemas.

Our professional disagreement

The more I worked with him, the lower the opinion I had of his professionalism. I deemed his accounting competencies quite partial and approximative. Similarly, his computer literacy was rather poor. In particular, his knowledge of Microsoft Excel was very basic. This, in turn, meant he had a very limited capacity to elaborate and analyze data.

With consistency, I radically improved the execution of the tasks that he delegated to me. Sometimes, it was just a streamlining of the procedure and the introduction of a more elaborate file. Other times, it meant the outright replacement of a practice that was not compliant with company or accounting's benchmarks.

I realized, one of the reasons why he was not supervising his own team was, quite simply, because he would have not known the best practices to apply. He relied heavily on his employees for the work to be done appropriately.

My approach was antithetical to his. I did possess specific knowledge about each function within our department. As such, I did proceed to implement a systematic rationalization of our office's practices. From one side, this gained me a public recognition by our Director of Finance. From the other, it sparked an instinctive fight back by a team that was not used to being kept in check.

My colleagues could not raise any exception about the rightfulness of the changes I was promoting. As such they did approach my manager to complain about the way I was introducing them. He, on the other hand, was very keen to grant them ground for their protest. His aim was clearly to weaken my position. My professional accomplishments were, in fact, under the eyes of the Director of Finance and other company executives. As a comparison to me, his own preparation was at risk to look mediocre.

Over time, our professional disagreement grew more and more into the open. It, actually, reached its peak in 2017. From one side, I was very keen to point out all the changes and improvements I had implemented over previous practices followed or approved by my manager; from the other, he seized every occasion to remind me of my poor popularity among our team.

Additional signs they could be together

Another month had passed, and we were now in autumn. Looking into the dating website I was a member of, I noticed Ms. S., previously a very regular user, suddenly disappeared from it. This was the pattern she had followed when the two of us got together. To me this was the sign she had now found another man.

Around the same time, my relationship with my manager cooled off considerably. We had never been close friends. Nevertheless, we used to go out for a drink after work time to time. We were also in touch on social media, and we had been out together occasionally. All of this now came to a halt.

The combination of these two events made my mind suspicious again and my anxiety hit paroxysm one more time. Of course, from one side I was tempted to link my manager's new attitude to the ongoing professional conflict that was taking place between the two of us. However, from the other I couldn't help but feel that this was the exact action he needed to take to free himself from any moral obligation toward myself and proceed to pursue a relationship with Ms. S.

Again, I found myself in a horrible state of anguish. I needed to know. I felt I still could have done something to stop their relationship from happening. Or, alternatively, I could have taken an action, like punching him in the face, that, even if it didn't bring her back to me, would have at least shown that no one could have disregarded my feelings without paying a price. I thought, somehow, this would have allowed me to retain some of my honor and respectability.

Observing my manager's behavior

Once more, I wanted to know. Once more, I didn't have a clear idea of how to achieve this objective. Furthermore, the fact that I did now lose a personal relationship with my manager made it awkward for me to address him any direct question concerning his private life. It looked like the only way I had to get to know something new about him was to keep my eyes and ears wide open at work.

One of the aims of this book is to reaffirm the priority of the fight for the survival of ourselves and our genes within our species and life in general. As a corollary of this thesis, human feelings depend foremost on the outcome of this struggle. We are happy when we feel we are winning or we think we have a good opportunity to achieve this objective in the future. We lay in anguish when we reckon we are failing. Each day every little experience we live is evaluated by our brain to the finality of natural selection: This swings our mood in one direction or another.

I observed my manager. He looked now genuinely upbeat and happy. This was a sharp contrast to six months before when after splitting up with his ex-girlfriend his mood was marred by sadness and resentment.

I came to know he was now going to the pub very rarely. He sharply cut off his drinking habit. Once, I overheard him talking with a colleague of ours about how he wanted to start a healthy diet and lose weight.

I could not feel happy for him. My mind was just deeply concerned about the reason that sparked all these radical changes.

A park close to her home

Some nights I could not sleep. I was very agitated. I used to go out for walks from time to time. They calmed me down.

One evening, I took the underground and went into Ms. S.'s area. I didn't want her to see me. I did not want her to worry. She had the right to leave me, and I wanted to respect that. I just needed to know if she was with my boss now.

Close to her place there was a park. When we were a couple, we had a habit of walking through it in the evening after she put her son to bed. I thought if she now had a partner, she would have walked through the park with him. I was wearing clothes that I never put on before. I hid my face with a hat. I remembered, along the perimeter of that park, there was a bench not lit up by the public lamps. From there, I could see all the people who were entering the area.

I was sitting on that bench around the time I used to walk with her. I waited there for approximately an hour. It was dark. I was constantly looking around. Very few people were out at that time. Mostly dog owners taking care of their pets. All of a sudden, a couple walked uphill on the opposite side of the road surrounding the park. Judging from how tall they were one could have been Ms. S. and the other my manager, but from that distance I couldn't identify them. They turned right to one of the residential areas. I rushed to the park's exit. I went to cross the road. A car motored fast toward me. I stopped just in time. I sprinted again. First straight, then uphill. When I reached the turning point, I couldn't see anybody in any direction.

I revisited the park two or three more times. I was not successful in any of these occasions.

Her birthday

Another month had passed. Ms. S.'s birthday was now up on the calendar.

Still, any thought of her was raising a great pain in me. On the other hand, when I managed to get a hold of my feelings, I was aware this recurrence would have provided me with a good opportunity to verify if she was now with my manager. Her birthday, indeed, was falling on a working Friday. I reasoned: If the two of them were together, I would have expected him not to be available that evening.

Acting upon this thought, on that day, I approached my manager and I invited him for a drink after work. He accepted. Once we were out, I wanted to make sure he was not due anywhere else later that day. I made up a story that my neighbors were organizing a party in my building that evening. I asked him if he was interested to join it with me. I was quite surprised to hear his positive reply to my offer. We carried on drinking for another half an hour. Then, I told him there was a change of plan and the party had been called off.

On my way home, that day, I felt relieved. Then I started to think again. Not even that occasion, indeed, had proven anything. Maybe, Ms. S. took a day off and had already flown back to her country to celebrate her birthday with her family and friends. If that was the case, my manager and her had probably celebrated this occurrence the evening before when, quite exceptionally, my manager left work significantly earlier than usual.

Would it matter if I knew?

At every moment, since I started my investigation, I was aware of its pettiness. I carried it out because, quite simply, I could not restrain myself. The most important matter was that I did not manage to keep Ms. S. on my side. She did not feel secure with me.

I had a look at my manager one more time. His manners were better than mine. After the difficult period that followed his last relationship, he succeeded in building up a new network of friends. Most of them were part of our company's management team. He was able to hold his own during conversations and this meant he was projecting an aura of security around him. People were seeking him, inviting him to parties.

This kind of strength was the one Ms. S. was looking for. So, in a way, it didn't really matter if they were together. What was significant was that they *could* have been together.

If I will ever be successful, it will not be in the same way of my manager. Yet, in being able to transcend my current status by getting stronger and being more effective lays all my hopes of any future happiness.

The winner

Life is complex. Most people don't have the education and the intelligence to seize it in this format. Our attention is drawn to visible handicaps without realizing, none of them, in itself, will determine our success or failure.

We face life as a bundle. All the characteristics we are made of interacts with the specific environment we are in. The actuality of this relation will dictate the outcome of our existence.

I believe life is always worth living. We can see patterns in our existence and in the environment that surrounds us until something unpredictable happens that makes us realize we didn't take into consideration all the variables involved, or we assigned them an incorrect weight, or both. We simply don't have the brain to account accurately for all of them.

On the eve of the fifth mass extinction, dinosaurs were ruling our planet. I would have not bet a cent on the rats.

CONCLUSION

The theory of evolution is science

The purpose of this book is to reaffirm the theory of evolution by means of natural selection as science. This implies that all its corollaries must be considered science too. The first of them is that failure is embedded in nature. It is not just a possibility: It is a necessity.

Happiness is not a right. Within each species, a certain number of individuals is destined to premature death and / or to not reproduce themselves. The only difference between varieties is the percentage of failing specimens between them. This is going to be low in more successful species, high in less thriving ones.

Statements like "There is space for everyone" or "No one will be left behind" are, indeed, false. The fact that these sentences have been thought and shared do not refute Darwin's theory. On the contrary, at a closer look, they are its very product. They are, in fact, nothing else than tools created to fight the natural struggle.

At an inter-species level, they are used to reassure and placate the losers in order to unify and strengthen our kind in its fight against others. Within our society, instead, they are alternately employed by a part to prevail on another. They are used by the winners to temper the insurgency of the losers; though, sometimes they are employed by the latter to ask the former to relax and share their grip on power and wealth.

The law of natural selection is the rightful lens to interpret our lives as well as all human history

The law of natural selection concerns the mechanisms through which each individual and species survive or perish. It is the fundamental law of life. As such, we cannot uphold it as science if we don't use it to interpret human existence both at a social as well as individual level.

All life is within the law of natural selection; none of it is outside this rule.

Darwin's principal is the rightful lens through which to examine and understand our personal experience as well as the whole of human history. It is the ultimate reason for each event to have happened. It is the criteria to which each random occurrence is related to and that provides reality with an order.

Culture is a tool

Culture is the elaboration of nature created by humankind. It is the particular tool our species has created to fight the struggle with all the other varieties and within itself.

Culture can be divided in three different sections according to their specific objectives: science and technology; morality and law; art.

Science and Technology. The purpose of this section is to enhance our collective and individual power by increasing our knowledge of nature and societies. We want to understand our environment to operate on it, to transform it at our own advantage.

At a general level, thanks to the advancements in these disciplines, we are ever increasing the amount of energy we harness from our surroundings, and we use it to sustain our species as well as to overpower all the others. Meantime, at a group and individual level, we want to use knowledge and tools created by science and technology to our benefit and at detriment of our opponents.

Morality and Law. This portion of human culture increases our collective and individual strength by regulating the relationships between humans. Its main objective is to promote behaviors and actions that increase our chances to survive and prosper individually and as a species. Equally, it is to censor and reprimand any deed that leads to achieve the exact opposite.

The first and most common social setting in which humanity thrives is one of reduced internal conflict. The reason for this is twofold. From one side, social peace ensures the energy of our species is not dissipated internally. From the other, it is the precondition for science and technology to flourish and to be passed on. Morality and law, therefore, will firstly support behaviors and actions aimed to minimize social struggle.

As in the case of science and technology, morality and law are also employed by social factions or individuals to prevail on their opponents. That is: We are constantly trying to mold these disciplines in a way that favor and promote our current status and condition.

<u>Art</u>. Art enhances our collective and individual prosperity by providing us with a second dimension in which to be successful. Art is the fictitious world. It is the environment we have created after our aspirations and desires have been shattered in our principal life. It is the domain to which we head to any time our day-to-day existence frustrates us. It is a space in which we recover and regroup. It is hope and opportunity, a second environment in which we can attempt our skills.

Art is a dimension autonomous from mundane reality. On the other hand, it entertains with it a dialectical relationship. This means that if we are effective in the former, our victory will reverberate into the latter. A winner in the world of art is successful altogether.

Morality and law: the concepts of good and evil

Morality and law maximize the chances of our species to survive and prosper as well as for the social group currently dominant within it through the promotion of a certain set of individual actions and the discouragement of others.

In order to achieve this result, these disciplines proceed to classify each human behavior or deed within two broad categories: one is labelled good, the other evil. Good actions are the ones that everyone should aim to realize any moment of their life. Evil deeds are the one that they should avoid.

Morality advocates for good undertakings and to refrain from evil ones through reasoning and persuasion. The law aims to achieve the same objective through the administration of extrinsic rewards and punishments.

Morality and law: regularity and evolution

Morality and law are used by humanity to increase its power over other kinds. At the same time, within societies, they are employed by a group of individuals to gain a bigger share of the wealth than the remaining ones.

These heterogenous forces exercise a constant pressure on these disciplines. This explains why they present both an element of regularity and evolution within themselves.

Morality and law are consistent because they promote the advancement of our species as a whole. What persistently strengthens a kind in opposition to others is a reduced internal conflict. For this reason, the actions that most endanger our social peace like murder and theft have consistently been condemned and punished across societies and over time.

On the other hand, morality and law have evolved over history to support the prosperity of a new dominant social group or to meet the challenges of a transformed environment. This explains why the same action has been branded as good or evil in different societies or at a different point in time. Just as an example, horse theft was punished with death in the Wild West. This was because the possession of a means of transportation was vital for the survival of the pioneers. Today the idea of killing a human being for the theft of an animal sounds abominable. What was once justice would now be viewed as crime.

Beyond good and evil

Good and evil are not primary elements. They are part of our culture. As such they are mere instruments to the promotion of our species. The absolute is the law of natural selection and our pursue of success. Society is not divided between good and bad people, but between fit and unfit individuals.

Morality and law maximize the number of people who will prosper within a specific society. Nevertheless, as dictated by the law of natural selection, there will always be a certain number of its members that will not achieve this objective.

A criminal is just an individual who has realized they will not be successful within the environment created by the law of the society they live in; equally, they have not resigned to lose.

An offender and their policeman (or any other non-criminal, for that matter) pursue the same objective: beating natural selection. The only difference between the two is that the latter is either achieving this result or is still confident they can do so within the confine of the law.

A criminal is just someone unfit to the environment they live in. The justice system, therefore, does not punish bad people: it sanctions the weak ones.

The Absolute

Culture is the particular elaboration of the environment created by human beings to fight natural selection. It is a proceeding of nature, not something different from it. As you would not think of a beehive or bird's nest as items that fall outside nature, so you should not consider human's culture as an autonomous dimension.

Humanity has got it all wrong. The Absolute is not in front of us as a separate entity that presides upon nature and our species. The Truth is behind us. It is in our roots, in our making. The Absolute is nature as the only entity and the one we belong to. There is nothing else than nature. Human culture, our words, our thoughts, our history, this book, are all the necessary shapes assumed by it.

Einstein's equation

I've always been fascinated by Einstein's equation: $E=mc^2$. The essence of this function is the statement that energy and mass are equivalent and interchangeable.

Yet, if we think about it, energy and mass are all that there is in the universe. That is: All that we can experience or detect falls in one of these two categories.

Consequently, if all that there is in the universe is mass and energy and they are equivalent and interchangeable, we will have to infer there is just one substance. Nature is one. There is nothing outside nature.

Space and movement

Nature is one. This is what Einstein's equation teaches us. It is one, but it is portioned in two interchangeable sections. These are the two dimensions that nature assumes.

There is a fundamental laceration in nature. This dichotomy is what has generated space and movement.

In Einstein's equation c is the space-time structure. The role that it is playing in his function is to be the balancing factor between energy and mass. That is: The space-time structure is necessary for these two entities to be distinct from one another. Equally, it is their division that generates c. Space and movement are a byproduct of the separation of energy and mass that occurred with the Big Bang.

Space-time sprang up from the Big Bang and the following division of nature into its two sub-sections. Before this event, we have to assume there was no space and movement.

The discrepancy

We live in a fractured and unstable universe. Its unity being lost with the Big Bang. Yet, within it, we detect processes that may eventually end its dichotomy.

Our universe is expanding at an accelerating rate. The mass of objects increases with speed. It is possible to foresee a time in which the mass of the cosmos will collapse. The gravitational force may, ultimately, dissolve the division between mass and energy. The universe would recover, in this scenario, its pre-Big Bang unity.

We are an expression of the post–Big Bang status of the universe. We don't know if the physical phenomena we currently witness will eventually collapse it and allow it to regain its uniformity. However, we do know that its "pre" status must have contained the forces—like an anti-gravity—that eventually led to the rupture of its equilibrium.

As far as it is our current knowledge, it is possible to understand nature as an entity that develop circularly.

Inert matter and life

The scientific mindset has come a long way. Yet, when we approach the subject of life, it still seems to lag. Our senses inform us there is noticeable difference between inert matter and life, so it is tempting to think of a divine-like intervention at the basis of the latter.

When we consider life, we always visualize something that grows or has self-motion. A sponge or a cork would not probably be the first thing that comes to our mind when we think about it.

I remember, when I was in school, I once saw a comparison between the atomic structure of a rock with that of a plant. What surprised me wasn't their differences; on the contrary, it was their similarities. The latter was definitely denser and more complex. Yet, I did not think the two were substantially alternative one to the other.

I see nature as a continuum of entities separated by a different complexity of their atomic structure. More atoms imply more energy. There isn't a jump between life and non-life. Every being is part of a spectrum.

Physical laws and biological laws

If we accept the idea that there is a linear progression between non-life and life, we will need to infer the laws that regulate the development of one will apply to the other and vice versa.

We already experience how physical laws affect living beings. What we don't perceive is the effects of biological laws on inert matter. This, though, does not substantiate the idea there are not. It could be their action on matter is weak and does not yield any measurable variation. Another possibility is that some physical laws and biological laws are, indeed, the same determination: We just cannot seize their identity as their proceedings on life and non-life are completely heterogenous.

Evolution by means of natural selection is a key biological law. However, if we recognize the homogeneity of life and non-life, we will also need to acknowledge this rule applies to the universe as a whole. Maybe it is the law that regulates its transformation. Maybe natural selection and entropy are the same regulation. At the moment we just don't have the understanding to acknowledge their identity.

A consideration over the question of the meaning of life

What is the meaning of life? This appears to be a fundamental question. I believe the best way to answer it is by making an analogy. Let's consider two queries. One is "What is the meaning of iron?" The other is "What is the meaning of the closed fist with the index and middle fingers raised?" In relation to the first sentence, we would probably answer that iron doesn't have any meaning. It simply is. With regard to the second—the peace sign—we would say that it is an invitation from a person to another to be amicable both within ourselves as well as in our relationship with others.

In order for a piece of iron to acquire a meaning, it needs to be worked upon by an intelligent being with the purpose to convey a message to another one.

This comparison teaches us meanings are never primordial. Significance was not born with the universe. It requires the development of intelligent beings and their will to communicate between each other. Meanings belong to culture not to nature.

Contents are created by intelligent beings, and they have validity just between them. They don't hold any importance within nature. The universe just is. We can assign to our lives any meaning we wish. It is not an absolute. That is: Independently from its answer, we have to acknowledge the question concerning the meaning of life is not a fundamental one. It doesn't really matter.

Criminality, addiction, loneliness, mental illness, and suicide

Social phenomena such as crime, addiction, loneliness, mental illness, and suicide will never be completely eradicated. This is because they spring up with the realization by some individuals, they are not going to be winners. According to the law of natural selection, in any given society, a certain number of subjects will not be successful. As the cause cannot be removed, so are its consequences. Being surprised by their presence or thinking they can be completely erased is just naïve, if not plainly foolish.

Social diseases cannot be entirely removed. However, they can be mitigated. This happens when the society we live in is reasonably equal and cohesive. In fact, we assess our performance in comparison with others. It is the stark difference that cause humiliation and pain and pushes us to extreme actions or damages us irreversibly.

Sociological studies around the world have proven this direct correlation between public distress and wealth inequality many times over. This is true when we compare different countries: Just think at the difference in criminality levels between reasonably equal societies like the Nordic countries and very unequal ones like the Latin American nations. However, this correlation is also demonstrated when we analyze the evolution of a single community over time. For instance, the rise in social malaise in in the United States in the last fifty years has mimicked its increase in wealth disparity over the same period of time.

Psychologists

Psychologists are useless. They are a group of pretentious individuals presiding upon non-scientific knowledge. They are not smart enough (even if most of them think they are) to produce a full picture of the phenomenon they have in front of them. They consider it just in its single manifestations. Because of this, the conclusions they draw are always partial and contradictory.

It is a popular opinion to equate psychologists to doctors: the latter treating the body and the formers the mind. Yet, there is a substantial difference between the two. An illness of the body is caused by a physical change that alters its correct functioning (a virus infection, a violent impact, etc.). As such, it is cured by an opposite corporal alteration aimed to recover our body's original balance.

The root cause of any mental illness is our subconscious realization we are not making the cut. The abruptness and the certainty with which we come to this understanding will determine the extension of our damage: from a simple neurosis to a partial or complete shutdown of our mind. The only true treatment of this disorder is to receive opposite feedbacks from reality. Being able to outsmart or overpower our social competitors. Receiving public acknowledgment for it.

As we all can understand, while a doctor can induce a physical change of our body, a psychologist cannot change our stand in society. This is something we need to do for ourselves.

As already stated, a mental illness is mitigated by time (assuming no further trauma occurs in the meanwhile). At this regard, a psychologist can provide two positive contributions to a patient's recovery. From one side, a therapist can be a solid reference for the sufferer while time works its effect. On the other, allowing the patient to talk about their trauma, assists them in objectivizing it and in reducing its pain. This, in turn, helps the sufferer to rationalize their experience and to work out a new life strategy. A professional's involvement, therefore, can help the patient to speed up their recovery.

In other words, a psychologist can offer to the patient the same help that a good friend would tender except that the latter would not charge us money and believe that any of our improvements are due to their intervention.

Non-hetero sexualities

I need to address non-hetero sexualities. It is commonly understood, in fact, that each individual is born in one of the many sexual orientations that are within humanity. There isn't a natural sexuality. This conception, of course, is in contradiction with the theory of natural selection that stands on the idea the objectives of life are equally self-preservation and reproduction.

This is the same conundrum of the champion of the weak ones. Did non-heterosexuals freely choose their sexuality or they have been forced into it?

Life is difficult. It is a continuous fight. This conflict reaches its pinnacle when we decide to have a partner and to form a family. From that moment onwards, we must be ready to protect and promote, not just ourselves, but our lineage too. Many of us realize (often after suffering a social defeat, a humiliation), they are not strong enough to sustain such a level of hostility. They avoid it, therefore, by changing their sexual orientation.

To abandon a heterosexual stand has got two principal consequences. First of all, it allows ourselves to withdraw from the mainstream part of society, where competition is at its peak. Secondly, it grants us the possibility to adopt a different morality from it. A much more flexible ethics in which the refusal to engage in the social conflict is not tainted by the same degree of shame.

Non-heterosexual people have renounced reproducing themselves in order to achieve self-preservation. This is the result of their own weakness. Nevertheless, as they still compete for their own life within society, they must stand strong and hide their flaws both to themselves and others. Hence, they state they either have been born with their sexual orientation or have freely chosen it. The advantage they gain from such a conception of sexuality is the same of an employee who, knowing that a promotion is not forthcoming, does not apply for it. They will not land the job, but at

Me after Ms. S.

I am not angry at Ms. S. I believe she genuinely granted me a chance and she hoped for our relationship to be successful. Clearly, she was not honest with me. She made me feel I was in a secure relationship while harboring many doubts about me. In the end, though, what matters is that I was not able to meet the challenges she put in front of me. If I did so, I am confident she would have not left me.

I have no doubt her rejection of me had nothing to do with my financial position. I am confident she will be a loving and faithful companion to the man she believes in and who makes her happy.

Of course, it would be easy to exonerate myself from any responsibility stating she was not the right woman for me. But I acknowledge how natural selection brings an element of absolutes within our society. We recognize the winners, and we are attracted to them.

Now it is up to me, one more time, to raise my game. I have to do it if I want to have any hope of happiness.

During the summer of 2017, I lost eight kilograms

of weight. I'm very proud of this but, at the same time, I vow to shed even more of it. I'm still overweight, after all.

I started to swim again. I go to the pool on Monday and Thursday.

In November 2017, I completed Level 1 of the CIMA qualification. I am very proud of this achievement too. The final exam was about applying a vast body of knowledge on specific situations within a restricted time. I had to think fast and correctly. Definitely one of the most difficult tests I had to sustain in my studies.

I wanted to start off the second level fast, but the writing of this book delayed my plan.

I also began to reduce my expenses and increase my savings. My finances don't look ideal in the long term. I will need to raise my income or further curtail my outgoings at a certain point in my future.

I really have a problem to get an uninterrupted sleep at night. I often wake up with a sweaty T-shirt and I have to change it. I think it is my conscience fearing I will not make the cut. This is very frustrating to me, as, I understand, it is a vicious circle. I need, in fact, a solid sleep to make sharp and effective decisions the following day. This is hampering my recovery.

I still don't know if Ms. S. and my manager are or have ever been together.

This book

All is within the law of natural selection. Nothing is outside it. Not even this book.

According to my division of culture, this work should be classified as art. It is something that I wrote after I suffered a major trauma in my life and as a way to diffuse my pain. It is, also, something I hope will be successful and the fortunes of which will reverberate in my principal life.

I author this book, in substance, to win.

When I was a young man, I wrote on the wall of my room: "Humanity speaks because it is suffering; if it were happy, it would remain silent." I thought about this sentence by reflecting on the sexual orgasm. This is the moment of maximum pleasure we can reach. It is characterized by a complete absence of desire. Within it, all is silent, all is motionless. After few moments, the balance is broken again. Noise, movement, time will start once more.

Space and movement stem from a fundamental dichotomy in nature. We take action, we write a book, we develop a culture because we are not happy. All our history is the product of our pain. If we were in balance, we would have probably never got out from the caves.

Now

It is 11pm. My book is finished. It is time for me to put my focus back on my main life. Tomorrow morning the alarm will ring. One after the other the challenges will come. I need to win as many fights as I can. I will need energy. I will need wit.

www.ingramcontent.com/pod-product-compliance
Lightning Source LLC
Chambersburg PA
CBHW030307100526
44590CB00012B/548